For my family,
friends and teachers
and for all those
who appreciate the beauty
of the Garden.

Most of the scripture verses are taken from the
New International Version, however, for the sake of poetry,
some passages are taken from the King James,
Revised Standard, Living Bible, New American and the
New American Standard.

Published by The C.R. Gibson Company,
Norwalk, Connecticut 06856
Printed in the United States of America
ISBN 0-8378-2502-4
GB2003

COME to the GARDEN

An Invitation to Serenity

By JoAnna O'Keefe
Illustrated by Helen Lea

The C.R. Gibson Company
Norwalk, Connecticut 06856

Introduction

I wrote, "Come to the Garden," at a time in my life when I was physically, emotionally and spiritually exhausted. I felt alone and defeated.

I remember calling my friend Ginger, and sobbing, "I feel like a broken pot of clay." She listened with a loving heart and answered softly, "I understand. Sometimes I feel I have poured myself out and there is nothing left." At that moment I knew I had to write—to sink into the depths of my feelings—and search for serenity.

As I wrote, tears of sorrow and despair dropped onto the blue lined paper and blurred the ink. I poured out my heart to the Lord, begging for relief, for solace, for peace. When I finished, the turbulence within was stilled and calm came over my spirit.

For two days I meditated, wanting to draw close to God, wanting to understand the mystery of suffering. Then, very gently, I was led to pick up my pen and write—"Quiet, quiet, quiet, my child, be still..."

It is my hope, that the meditations in this simple book will lead you to the Garden, that quiet place within, where God speaks in a whisper and miracles happen.

JoAnna O'Keefe

Lord,

I feel fragmented

Like a broken pot of clay.

I've lost my focus;

I've lost my way.

Give me relief from my distress;
be merciful to me and hear my prayer.

Psalms 4:1

Out of the depths I cry to you,
O Lord;
O Lord, hear my voice.
Let your ears be attentive
to my cry for mercy.

Psalms 130:1-2

I am like a broken vessel.

Psalms 31:12

I've

poured myself out.

I'm drained, I'm dry;

I sense a discontent

I can't identify.

...my soul is poured out within me;
days of affliction have taken hold of me.

Job 30:16

My strength has dried up
like sun-baked clay...
        Psalms 22:15

How Long, O Lord?
Will you forget me forever?
How long will you hide your face from me?
How long must I wrestle with my thoughts
and every day have sorrow in my heart?
        Psalms 13:1- 2

feel rootless

Like rolling tumbleweed,

Moving, moving, moving,

Dizzy, from the speed.

I have no peace, no quietness;
I have no rest, but only turmoil.
Job 3:26

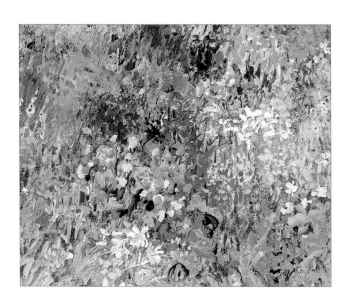

My days are swifter than a runner;
they fly away without a glimpse of joy.

Job 9:25

The churning inside me never stops;
days of suffering confront me.

Job 30:27

feel like quitting.

I feel self-doubt.

I'm tired, Lord,

I'm worn out.

My soul is in anguish.
How long, O Lord, how long?

Psalms 6:3

I am worn out with pain;
every night my pillow is wet with tears.

Psalms 6:6

I am utterly helpless,
without any hope.

Job 6:13

How

can I integrate

My scattered thoughts,

My dreams?

How can I find balance,

Freedom from extremes?

My days have passed,
my plans are shattered,
and so are the desires of my heart.

Job 17:11

...everything is futility
and striving after wind.

Ecclesiastes 2:17

Where shall wisdom be found?
And where is the place of understanding?

Job 28:12

How

can I slow down?

How can I release?

There are so many pressures.

How can I find peace?

*Come, Lord, and show me your mercy,
for I am helpless,
overwhelmed, in deep distress.*

Psalms 25:16

Show me the path where I should go, O Lord;
point out the right road for me to walk.

Psalms 25:4

O Lord, be not far off;
O my Strength, come quickly to help me.

Psalms 22:19

Be still, and know that I am God.

Psalms 46:10

quiet, quiet,

My child, be still.

Listen to your feelings.

Discipline your will.

LET NOT your heart be troubled.

John 14:1

I am the way, the truth, and the life.

John 14:6

Everything is possible to one who has faith.

Mark 9:23

ome

to the Garden,

The secret place we share.

My essence is in the Garden;

Come to Me in prayer.

I will not leave you desolate;
I will come to you.
John 14:18

Come to me...and I will give you rest.
                              Matthew 11:28

When you pray, go into your inner room.
                              Matthew 6:6

Ask and it will be given to you;
seek and you will find;
knock and the door will be opened to you.
                              Matthew 7:7

Transcend

worldly cares.

Seek the kingdom first.

Peace lies within;

It is for Me you thirst.

*Where your treasure is,
there your heart will be also.*
Luke 12:34

The kingdom of God is within you.
Luke 17:21

My peace I give to you;
not as the world gives do I give to you.
Let not your heart be troubled,
neither let it be afraid.
John 14:27

Whoever drinks the water I shall
give will never thirst.
John 4:13

*A*ccept

your limitations;

Embrace humility.

Here lies the path to wisdom

And to maturity.

The tree is known by its fruit.
Matthew 12:33

My grace is sufficient for you,
for my power is made perfect in weakness.

IICorinthians 12:9

Whoever exalts himself will be humbled,
and whoever humbles himself will be exalted.

Matthew 23:12

Come

to the Garden,

The soul's sweet bouquet.

The flowers of tomorrow

Are in the seeds of today.

Don't be anxious about tomorrow.
...Live one day at a time.

Matthew 6:34

Consider the lilies, how they grow;
they neither toil nor spin, yet I tell you,
even Solomon in all his glory
was not arrayed like one of these.

Luke 12:27

Together

we will weed.

Together we will sow.

Together we will water.

Together, you will grow.

These things I have spoken to you,
that my joy may be in you,
and that your joy may be full.

John 15:11

Remain in me, and I will remain in you.
No branch can bear fruit by itself;
it must remain in the vine. Neither
can you bear fruit unless you remain in me.

John 15:4

If you remain in me
and my words remain in you,
ask whatever you wish,
and it will be given to you.

John 15:7

COME to the GARDEN

Lord, I feel fragmented
Like a broken pot of clay.
I've lost my focus;
I've lost my way.

I've poured myself out.
I'm drained, I'm dry;
I sense a discontent
I can't identify.

I feel rootless
Like rolling tumbleweed,
Moving, moving, moving,
Dizzy, from the speed.

I feel like quitting.
I feel self-doubt.
I'm tired, Lord,
I'm worn out.

How can I integrate
My scattered thoughts,
My dreams?
How can I find balance,
Freedom from extremes?

How can I slow down?
How can I release?
There are so many pressures.
How can I find peace?

An Invitation to Serenity

By JoAnna O'Keefe

Quiet, quiet, quiet,
My child, be still.
Listen to your feelings.
Discipline your will.

Accept your limitations;
Embrace humility.
Here lies the path to wisdom
And to maturity.

Come to the Garden,
The secret place we share.
My essence is in the Garden;
Come to Me in prayer.

Come to the Garden,
The soul's sweet bouquet.
The flowers of tomorrow
Are in the seeds of today.

Transcend worldly cares.
Seek the kingdom first.
Peace lies within;
It is for Me you thirst.

Together we will weed.
Together we will sow.
Together we will water.
Together, you will grow.

Colophon

Editor: Julie Mitchell
Graphic Designer: Aurora C. Lyman

Type set in Shelley Allegro Script
Garamond Book and Simoncini Garamond Italic